THE LOVES
OF
SHAKESPEARE'S WOMEN

THE LOVES
OF
SHAKESPEARE'S WOMEN

Susannah York

London
NICK HERN BOOKS
www.nickhernbooks.co.uk

A Nick Hern Book

The Loves of Shakespeare's Women
first published in Great Britain in 2001 by Nick Hern Books Ltd
14 Larden Road, London W3 7ST.

The Loves of Shakespeare's Women © 2001 by Susannah York

Susannah York has asserted her moral right to be identified
as the author of this work

Jacket photograph: Richard Mildenhall
Jacket design: Ned Hoste, 2H

Typeset by Country Setting, Kingsdown, Kent CT14 8ES
Printed and bound in Great Britain by Biddles, Guildford

British Library Cataloguing data for this book
is available from the British Library

ISBN 1 85459 639 X

To Sasha and Orlando

who first said it was a 'goer'

Contents

PART TWO: MID YEARS AND BEYOND

Acknowledgements

To all the names mentioned in the preface,
I owe a debt of gratitude and of affection.
Every one of them was extraordinarily
generous with encouragement, time,
knowledge, inspiration or practical help
from the start or along the way.

Others have gone unsung – my own
personal technical wizard Lawrence Charles
who, time after time, and never complaining,
sorted out problems with my laptop and
taught me to regard it as a friend . . .
Anna Mackmin, my early choice as the show's
director, too busy, but urging onwards, and
Matthew Warchus for being my means to her . . .
old friend Stanley Corngold from Princeton
University, who read and suggested when
Hungarian and Georgian dust had settled . . .
and Anthony Fabian, another comrade-in-arms
always big on encouragement, who propelled
me towards Carl Miller.

More recently Jo Luke of the Royal Court
Theatre has given me invaluable help in trying
to ensure that the show has a future. And
I know – come Edinburgh Festival time –
I'm going to feel very glad of Mary Shields
and Richard Hull, who will produce the show
at the Assembly Rooms.

Finally there's Nick Hern who flew a kite,
persuading me that a show could have another
life and become a book . . . I never thought
I'd find an editor in the class of Maureen Rissik
but I did, and he's published it too.

Note on Sources

For my textual sources I have drawn mainly
from the Oxford University Press *Works of
Shakespeare* and in part from the Arden
Shakespeare, the Penguin Shakespeare, and
Dent's 'New Temple Shakespeare'.

Scenes have been edited in certain cases to
create monologues and occasionally, where
I felt it appropriate, another's word, or words,
put in the protagonist's mouth. This – and
sometimes my own sensing of the text – has
inevitably led to some variation in punctuation.

Shakespeare and Company

My first solo performance happened by accident.
I'd been set to direct Susan Hampshire in Cocteau's
La Voix Humaine, then our dates conflicted, and
I jumped in to replace her. (Waste my new trans-
lation?! That had been an accident too: we'd found
the original dated.) One endless, grief-stricken hour
with a silent telephone as co-star. That first night in
Bromley, and on many more, in different countries
over several years – I thought, 'How can anyone
bear the *loneliness*? Never again!'

Alone-ness is at the heart of *The Human Voice*,
a woman on her last desperate call to the lover who
has dumped her, but it's inherent, that loneliness of
a one-person show. All the same, I tried it again in
Mark Davies Markham's funny/sad *Independent
State*, tale of a would-be country-western singer,
though I had Sam, a laughing guitarist, to keep me
in tune: and yet again in Brian McAvera's *Picasso's
Women* as the grieving, manipulative, last wife,
Jacqueline, with only her conjurings of the altogether
absent Picasso to people the stage.

And then suddenly here I was *again* – for this book
was born out of yet another one-person show, and
it, *The Loves of Shakespeare's Women*, came about
not by accident, but by my own devising.

How did it all, book, show, book-of-the-show, begin?

My friend Richard Jackson, producer of those first
two plays, gave me kick-starts over the years. 'Time
for another!', or did I want to reprise? I remembered
the loneliness, was reluctant, read one-person
plays . . . dallied.

Katalin Bogyay, director of the Hungarian Cultural
Centre, made encouraging noises. 'If you have an
idea . . . something classical? Want to try it out in
the Centre . . . '

And then came media reports that Shakespeare was
to be omitted from the state school curriculum.
I suddenly had a subject I cared about.

The title of John Gielgud's Shakespeare show *The
Ages of Man* came to mind. Why not an *Ages of
Woman*, I thought, and had a coat-hanger.

And as I assembled and chose my women, I discovered
my theme.

*

Touring in a play can create the perfect conditions
for writing. A kind of limbo exists, time off, time
to be *yourself*, not somebody's something, mother
or daughter or mate; you're at a brief remove from
home-tasks, family, friends, even sometimes a
telephone. The flip side of touring is that, no matter
how well you get on with your cast, 'digs' or B&Bs
can be lonely places, and when it's raining or cold
you don't necessarily want to see sights or walk on
a neighbouring hill. Yet there are these whole
daytimes to fill! And for a pen-pushing actor on
tour, the proverbial solitariness of writing is
marvellously alleviated when you act at night with

your fellows, scramble to the pub after the show, share jokes in the dressing-rooms, a company meal, a company jaunt, or insights born out of playing to new audiences, or of your own growing familiarity with the play.

Last year I toured Britain through late winter and spring with a company of six. And I had my day-time idea. Range is implied whenever Shakespeare is in the title, and as the show evolved and took its structure, that 'range-ing' was hugely exciting – the choosing, the *being* of these women, even embryonically as I tested them out, then editing and writing the linking passages . . . And it gave huge headaches, too. This plethora of marvellous women! I wanted to do them all. But of course there'd be restrictions of time, of my own ability to hold all these women, of an audience's will to digest them. Inevitably I would end up with a list of 'Possibles', characters I thought I might one day interchange with some in the original structure. These 'Possibles' are included at the end of the book.

The tour ended, and I started tentatively to learn, taking my evolving script and laptop to a Greek island. Locals were mystified as Viola's joy echoed through olive groves, Constance's grief swelled Ionian seas, but everyone knew who Juliet was. English friends on the island generously listened; Ruscha suggested Emilia, Sally an alternative Beatrice which I added to my list of 'Possibles' . . . Home again, and urged on by the indefatigable Katalin, I committed myself, almost sleep-walking towards a 'work-in-progress' evening in late

September at the Hungarian Centre. Then I put my Shakespearean women away to concentrate on Picasso's last, Jacqueline, for the Edinburgh Festival.

*

Hungary, Hungarians, had a lot to do with making the show a reality. In Edinburgh I met Laszlo Magacs, director of the Merlin Theatre in Budapest. A protégé of Peter Brook, he was trawling for shows, liked the script. There was space for a couple of performances in October ('All Hungarians know Shakespeare, our Vilmos'), he'd come to the 'work-in-progress' . . . In Edinburgh I met too, the marvellous and overwhelming Keti Dolidze, a Georgian actress who was performing her own one-woman show. 'Budapest', she cried, 'in October?' Why not hop on eastwards to play the Festival in Tbilisi? ('All Georgians know Shakespeare, our Ouiliam . . . '). I had no director, no music, no lights, and a scarily short time to find them or learn my text. I said yes.

From early on, my cartoonist friend Richard Willson had been a patient and generous sounding-board, turning up odd felicitous phrases as I struggled with my links. But professional input was what I needed, and with performances of *Picasso's Women* taking me up till September 10th, no director I trusted was available.

Then Laszlo e-mailed. Subject to liking the 'work-in-progress', he would lend me his theatre, his 'eye', his lighting designer, his composer/pianist for a few days before the two performances in Budapest. Needing the 'eye' though, now, a mind and an ear too, with three weeks to go I started on a wing and a prayer to rehearse.

I'd had a brilliant idea – Andrew Bone! Boney is an actor-friend of my son Orlando; I'd watched them perform together that season at the RSC. Imaginative, funny, open, well-versed in Shakespeare and with perfect confidence in his own judgement, and an astonishing technical expertise, Boney proved the perfect collaborator.

We'd rehearse in my open-plan kitchen/sitting-room. Boney would straddle a stool in the kitchen bit, glasses perched, watch, listen, question; jump up with an idea, turn another on its head. 'All right, you do it!' I'd say from my up-three-steps where I'd been perorating. And he would, brilliantly. When the sun was out, we'd rehearse in the garden to the neighbours' amazement – or amusement perhaps, since they're used to it. Sometimes he'd chortle, talk like the clappers, sometimes he'd be quite silent. What I remember most about those rehearsals was the sheer fun we had in discovering these women, the exchange of ideas, the freedom I felt to make a fool of myself, and the joy of trusting this friend of Orlando's, who'd become mine too.

*

And it was in those days I made my best discovery.

Boney voiced it. We'd had the first run. He jumped up, babbling. 'It's so exciting seeing them all together – as you went on from one to another, I had the sense of the early ones, Juliet and Rosalind, Cressida and Beatrice crowding the wings, waiting for whoever'd come next.'

There they all were, I'd felt them too, cheering on Cleopatra, Emilia, Queen Margaret, colouring them with their own pasts. How was I going to feel *lonely*?

We were careering towards September 30th.

I'd talked to an early music enthusiast, Harry Booth, who unburrowed for me familiar and unfamiliar themes; his daughter, my old friend Angie endlessly encouraging, helped me time them and tape them, and together we found others. A young Russian designer, Olga Maximenkova, who'd done wonders for my fringe production of *Eugene Onegin*, translated my vague imaginings into white tunic and white satin pants for the cross-dressing heroines, the young ones; a long red satin dress (*velvet* one day, I think) for the older, richer women. We dreamed up different coloured scarves, blue for Viola, green for Rosalind, purple for Isabella and Portia, a blight orange-red for Beatrice and Katharina: Cleopatra's would be gold or peacock blue, Lady M. would don a black cloak, the Merry Wives autumnal red-brown linen (a pink bonnet for Alice?), Mistress Quickly a cap . . . and they'd gather, these garments once worn, and lie in a heap on the stage, small incarnations, while their ghosts stacked the wings.

But the scarves didn't get made. September 30th had come.

*

The Hungarian Cultural Centre in Covent Garden is a huge oak-floored room with a magnificent Victorian fireplace; it seats sixty. Katalin allowed us to light the 'stage' with huge candelabra, throw a mock-medieval tapestry over the fireplace. I didn't trust myself to know my 'links', so rewritten they had been as I struggled for concision (and why is one's own stuff so much harder to learn than Shakespeare's . . . ?) so I borrowed a lectern – and from my kitchen a high wooden stool, from a friend a 'rustic' bench. Boney would manage the mysteries of the mini-disc system.

And the first work-in-progress happened.

The room was stuffed with warm Hungarians, friends of Katalin, and just as warm friends of mine and Boney's – Ruscha, and Angie, the two Richards, Sasha my daughter, son Orlando, American Erik who never stops urging me to write, Chrissie, Lindy, Dedie, writer Carl Miller who'd read the first version . . . made suggestions . . . and would afterwards send me a marvellously useful critique.

It was very hot. And very scary. They were so close! And I could see them! My eyes would land on an encouraging face in the middle of a link, what should I do, engage? Yes of course, but oh then, wouldn't I lose my thread? I did, but they smiled and clapped and the interval came and I rushed off to change into satin. Katalin poured wine for the audience, Boney popped in with a grin to my 'dressing-room', then off we set again, with all the just-past, the Shakespearean young ones, thronging the 'stage' and urging the older ones on.

Next day, Ninon, one of the audience and a recent friend, telephoned from the King's Head, one of London's earliest fringe theatres. I'd worked there twice, and that week, she said, the theatre had a couple of free nights and its friendly founder Dan Crawford was offering me one or both at no charge, for further 'work-in-progress'. The programme of the current play, *Ring Round the Moon*, could be 'slipped', she said; it was short notice of course, but might garner a small, non-paying audience. And there was just time before I left for Hungary.

I leapt at the bounty. Boney enthusiastically concurred, and two days later we moved onto the tiny but real stage with its French-garden set. There was no space for a lectern so I sat on a balustrade, and we created a modest lighting plot among the leaves, playing to assorted locals, and friends who'd previously slipped through the net. Afterwards we made a collection for my Israeli hero, Mordechai Vanunu, then I flew to Budapest.

*

The Merlin is a modern theatre with a mid-European feel; it frequently puts on plays in English. The stage is deep, wide, with a raked auditorium seating perhaps two hundred, three times as many as the Hungarian Centre or the King's Head. Changes to the show would include some 're-blocking' and Laszlo would create a real lighting plot, but the biggest innovation was to be a grand piano onstage, upon which Ferenc Darvas – 'Feri' – would improvise at certain, to-be-worked-out moments. The idea terrified me. Feri with his minimal English turned out to be a fey, enchanting presence – but Boney and I'd so recently sorted timings to strains

18

of lute and harpsichord! How was this improvising Hungarian pianist going to create the sounds of Shakespeare? Four days to re-learn . . . then un-learn, because Tbilisi would have no Feri and I'd be back to the mini-disc again.

Ferenc Darvas is a superb, delicate musician who'd uncannily catch the moment when his sound would underscore, not intrude on, the text – catch the mood of that moment, making his own 'Shakespearean' music which you'd swear came not from a piano but a harpsichord. I threw preconceptions to the wind, and myself into the short, extraordinary joy of working with these two Hungarians.

Laszlo wanted me to abandon the lectern altogether. 'Too formal,' he insisted. 'This is a private evening with you. It's you we want, not a Shakespeare lesson between' – much as Carl Miller had said, reading my first draft script 'I want you, Susannah, a bit more of you there!' Fearful then, of seeming vain, even more, of giving myself away (what after all, was my experience in Shakespeare?) I'd argued wasn't I there enough already, in my choices, in the way I'd do them? . . . Anecdotes? I didn't have any. 'Trawl,' Carl said, so I did. My friend Kenneth Haigh had sworn 'I couldn't do it! Reveal myself? Fair enough, the acting bit, but you'll have to give *yourself* too, you're the subject.' 'But the subject is Shakespeare!' 'No, no, you're both in there,' he'd said. Director, writer, actor, all nudging me towards generosity to the audience, generosity with myself, and only the shy actor understanding how difficult that is to do.

And that was when I understood how different this exercise was. *La Voix Humaine*, *Independent State*, *Picasso's Women* are plays. I was being someone else from start to finish, and a lonely, frightening, if often exciting, business it had felt. This was even scarier, leaping in and out of skins, so many different skins! then being me, just me, in between. But I remembered how the gathering women, live ghosts, would collect in the wings to urge me and the rest of them on.

That Laszlo Magacs was entrepreneurial I'd already discovered, and more than a hint anarchic. As a director he proved humorous, inventive, wonder-fully practical, and I trusted his 'eye' at once. We rummaged among the Merlin Theatre's props, found a period throne-like chair, a pedestal, a fibre-glass 'Grecian' block to replace the bench, a tall candelabra I'd light. There was another chair, and a table where I could set my 'safety-blanket', the script, stage right.

Laszlo had definite ideas on the characters of the women, most of which fortunately accorded with mine and Boney's. Time was short and he suggested only two or three radical changes, all of them valuable, but in such a large space some of the pieces, the characters, needed new choreography. We'd rehearse, he, me, and Feri, for a few hours each day onstage, then – while he went off to devise the ingenious lighting-plot, cast *A Midsummer Night's Dream* and tend to the running of his theatre – I'd continue alone on-stage or set off for my magnificent 'digs' across the way, the Astoria, to work in the huge, beautiful, sun-filled room with its balcony reaching out towards leaves turned orange, trees beginning to bare . . . On the fourth of these Hungarian Indian summer days, Richard Jackson, who would produce the next lap of the show, joined me; and Laszlo drove us to Vienna from where we caught a 'plane to Tbilisi. It was the morning of October 15th.

Tbilisi, Georgia! We were met late afternoon by an ebullient Keti Dolidze with flowers – and with television cameras, reporters, flash-bulbs, which dismayed me who, used to the working atmosphere of London and Budapest, had arrived in jeans. The warmth of the welcome could not have been exceeded, but a further shock was in store. As we were whisked to our hotel, a simple 17th-century merchant house on a cobbled street with wonderful views of town and hills, Keti asked sweetly if I'd mind following the Festival's opening ceremony with the show on the morrow at five, not waiting to play the night after, as planned. (Unfortunately, she added, we wouldn't be able to see the theatre till morning. It was locked up.)

I reeled . . . Agreed. And with a rather desperate sense of 'in for a penny, in for a pound' and tossing my bonnet over windmills, joined Keti, Richard, leading Georgian, and visiting Russian, actors, artists, and dignitaries at a huge, delicious Georgian dinner in a restaurant that might once have been an old railway waiting room. Again came that marvellous welcome, that infectious joy at our being there. But my sense of doom was deepening: almost nobody but Keti spoke English. No time to cut, to re-jig. How were they going to cope, this tomorrow's audience, with seventy-odd minutes of Shakespeare and twenty or so of York? 'All Georgians know Shakespeare, our Ouiliam . . . '

They coped. They were in fact, heroic – utterly attentive and chuckling even, at the odd, visually comic moment. Keti and her team had worked overtime in the morning to find props, put up lighting states in this town where black-outs are the norm. And so, shortly after five and almost comatose with terror, there I was playing on a raised stage to the packed theatre and strains of a mini-disc lute.

I went slow first, for clarity – then in mounting panic, raced. A local theatre director said 'I know the Shakespeare, I like the sound, I cannot understand of course, the English. Did she breathe? I watched, I watched very hard for a breath . . . ' Heroic – and generous. They sent me home unwarrantably richer for a Giacometti-like bronze of their national theatrical hero inscribed 'Susannah York. For excellence in Art'. Art, the Georgian thing . . . art, and independence. After my too few days in this rich, poor, theatre-crammed city, days of watching plays, films, walking through medieval churches full of frescoes and icons, of meeting painters, sculptors, poets, actors, musicians, film-makers, of seeing Keti's and others' dedication to the Festival, I carried away a deep sense of that Georgian love of art, of the arts. Carried that away, and the absolute certainty that I must create a short, one-hour version of my show if I wanted to travel my Shakespeare women.

Laszlo, who had viewed the Georgian adventure with scepticism, even alarm ('You never know with those airlines'), met us back in Budapest with undisguised relief, and we set to work with only three days to prepare for the preview. Three days of 'tech'ing – of re-learning the size of the stage, altered moves, new lighting cues, above all of learning to work again with fey, fantastical, free-wheeling Feri.

And so came about what counts, I suppose, as the first professional performance – a 'preview' before mainly English-speaking or at least Shakespearean-acquainted drama students, actors, and a loyal Merlin-going public. At the end I grabbed Feri's hand, dragged him downstage, and spoke the first four lines of Puck's epilogue to him 'If we shadows have offended . . . ', and he smiled, nodding and bobbing like one of the midsummer fairies, as if Puck were speaking his tongue. And the following night when we played to the British Council and new possible sponsors of the Merlin, calm, wry, risk-taking Laszlo was touchingly nervous, whispering backstage as he wished me luck, 'I think I'm more frightened than you!'

One more performance. Laszlo had been a little sheepish about this. The American School outside Budapest had requested three master-classes from me the following morning, to be followed by a late matinee performance in their theatre.

The primary-class, who'd all watched the *Superman* video as a sort of (self-set) homework, gustily improvised – a wonderfully inventive group of 'hams' they were, who leapt on my suggestions like gannets, then flung themselves back into their situations and characters with ever more abandon.

The sessions with the mid- and late-teens were more problematic (why do we grow more self-conscious every year we grow on?) The mids had prepared short scenes which they took a great deal of persuading to perform. Finally, a Viola at odds with her best friend, the Olivia, for winning the favour, as it transpired, of their Orsino, was coaxed into playing – after which there was an avalanche of 'Us next!'s, and argument because time had run out. The late-teens simply wanted to be entertained with stories about Marlon Brando.

Then I saw the 'theatre'. It was a huge eight-hundred-or-so seater hall, perfect for Speech-Day, conferences, graduation, but oh, for my *one-person show* . . . ? Laszlo had recreated a fair facsimile of the Merlin lighting-plot, but there'd be no chance to rehearse on this hugely aggrandised stage. Well, in for a penny . . .

The performance was around five-thirty. By the time I'd been brought back from a lulling lunch with Hungarian wine and the headmaster in a sunny, leaf-strewn square, most of the pupils had scarpered back to Budapest on the school-bus. Some sixty or seventy unfortunates though, had been collared by staff, (detention?), or by 'schoolrun' parents persuaded they were in for some culture, and these had scattered themselves in isolated pockets across the vast auditorium.

Summarily deciding to dump Cressida, Lady M., Mistress Quickly, I donned white tunic, white pants, and imaginary seven-league boots. Crunch of crisps, rustle of sweet-papers, slurping noises of cokes and ices (this was a well-stocked school), snorts, giggles, grumbles, and 'shushes' reached me in the wings as miles across the stage I saw Feri twinkling . . . Then he started to play, the lights went down, came up – and Juliet, Rosalind, Beatrice and the rest came tumbling onto the stage with me . . .

In for a pound.

May 2001

THE LOVES
OF
SHAKESPEARE'S WOMEN

PART ONE
Youth

SONNET XVIII

Shall I compare thee to a summer's day?
Thou art more lovely and more temperate:
Rough winds do shake the darling buds of May,
And summer's lease hath all too short a date:
Sometime too hot the eye of heaven shines,
And often is his gold complexion dimm'd:
And every fair from fair sometime declines,
By chance, or nature's changing course untrimm'd;
But thy eternal summer shall not fade,
Nor lose possession of that fair thou ow'st,
Nor shall death brag thou wander'st in his shade
When in eternal lines to time thou grow'st;
   So long as men can breathe, or eyes can see,
   So long lives this, and this gives life to thee.

Introduction

Jacques in 'As You Like It' charts the 'seven ages' of a man's life, and it was Gielgud's one-man evening 'The Ages of Man' which triggered this show. 'Why not an "Ages of Woman"?' I thought and went delving into Shakespeare. But . . . 'infant mewling and puking'? 'whining schoolgirl'? Queen Lear? It was no good being literal.

What a ragbag of colours though!

Passionate women, comic women jostled; subtle women, savage, submissive or scheming, young and old, joyful, grieving, from every kind of background. Familiar themes emerged – the fleeting nature of beauty and life, personal values evoked beyond 'a little brief authority', man as an ape – and the gender question: tease of the sonnets and manifest in the plays with their cross-dressing and role-swapping.

But in my jostling ragbag was there one, uniting thread? What would this show be about?

Romeo and Juliet

*In a tender, impatient soliloquy the newly-wed
young Juliet evokes night, and Romeo: my first
challenge at drama school, in our second week.*

*One of the soliloquies, and the balcony scene –
we've been told to learn both, we have to do
one or the other. Rigid with terror I've been
slipping my Romeo peppermints in case.
(Please not the soliloquy, don't make me be
on my own! So Tom Thingummy's got bad
breath, but I don't want to get up alone.)*

*Our tutor scrutinises his register. 'Right then.
We'll start at the wrong end of the alphabet . . .
York. And, yes, the soliloquy, I think.'*

*We who are about to die . . . I stagger up on
stage in front of thirty budding actors whose
names I've yet to learn.*

*The tutor seems to be making vaguely porno-
graphic faces.*

*'Astound us, Susannah. Come on now, be sexy!
Fourteen, and it's your wedding-night, can't
wait for it, right?'*

Gallop apace, you fiery-footed steeds
Towards Phoebus' lodging; such a waggoner
As Phaëton would whip you to the west
And bring in cloudy night immediately.
Spread thy close curtain, love-performing night!
That runaways' eyes may wink, and Romeo
Leap to these arms, untalk'd of and unseen!
Lovers can see to do their amorous rites
By their own beauties; or, if love be blind,
It best agrees with night. Come, civil night,
Thou sober-suited matron, all in black,
And learn me how to lose a winning match,
Play'd for a pair of stainless maidenhoods:
Hood my unmann'd blood, bating in my cheeks,
With thy black mantle; till strange love, grown bold,
Think true love acted simple modesty.
Come, night! Come, Romeo! come thou day in night!
For thou wilt lie upon the wings of night,
Whiter than new snow on a raven's back.
Come, gentle night: come, loving, black-brow'd night
Give me my Romeo: and when he shall die,
Take him and cut him out in little stars,
And he will make the face of heaven so fine
That all the world will be in love with night
And pay no worship to the garish sun.
O! I have bought the mansion of a love,
But not possess'd it, and though I am sold
Not yet enjoy'd. So tedious is this day
As is the night before some festival
To an impatient child that hath new robes
And may not wear them. O! here comes my nurse,

And she brings news; and every tongue that speaks
But Romeo's name speaks heavenly eloquence!

Romeo and Juliet, Act III, Scene 2

*Romantic love infuses Shakespeare's youth.
And I suddenly saw that it's love that strings
together all these women, from Juliet to
Mistress Ford, Isabella to Constance – love in
its many natures, aspects, objects. Romantic
love, yes. And* family *love – sibling-, cousin-,
parental love. Love for your master, for your
mistress, for your comrade, for your country.
Love of power, of God, of fun, of an abstract
ideal . . . returned love, misplaced love, love
that betrays, love that stays, love that's turned
awry.*

*Love it is that strings these women on a single
thread, and that's what the show is about.*

Twelfth Night

*Viola cross-dressed as a boy, has become page
to the Duke Orsino with whom she has fallen
in love – and he himself is in love with the
beautiful, disdaining Olivia.*

*Sent by Orsino with a letter from which she
quotes, to woo the lady on his behalf, Viola
hotfoots to her rival's house and comes upon
Olivia there, veiled amongst her quarrelling
entourage.*

VIOLA

The honourable lady of the house, which is she?

'Most radiant, exquisite, and unmatchable beauty – '

I pray you tell me if this be the lady of the house,
for I never saw her: I would be loath to cast away
my speech; for, besides that it is excellently well
penned, I have taken great pains to con it. Good
gentle one, give me modest assurance if you be the
lady of the house, that I may proceed.

I am a messenger. I bring no overture of war, no
taxation of homage, I hold the olive in my hand;
my words are as full of peace as matter.

'Most sweet lady, – ' Good madam, let me see
  your face!

Excellently done, if God did all . . .

'Tis beauty truly blent, whose red and white
Nature's own sweet and cunning hand laid on:
Lady, you are the cruell'st she alive
If you will lead these graces to the grave
And leave the world no copy.
My lord and master loves you; O, such love
Could be but recompensed, though you were crowned
The nonpareil of beauty!
With adorations, with fertile tears,
With groans that thunder love, with sighs of fire –
If I did love you in my master's flame,
With such a suff'ring, such a deadly life,
In your denial I would find no sense,
I would not understand it.
                    Why, what would I? . . .
Make me a willow cabin at your gate,
And call upon my soul within the house
With loyal cantons of contemned love,
And sing them loud even in the dead of night;
Holla your name to the reverberate hills,
And make the babbling gossip of the air
Cry out 'Olivia!' O, you should not rest
Between the elements of air and earth,
But you should pity me!

Twelfth Night, Act I, Scene 5

A Midsummer Night's Dream

*I was mortified not to be cast as Shylock, or
even Portia in my school's first Shakespeare
production – but the following summer-term
came my more-than-compensation, Puck in the
open air. Euphoria!*

*I love 'A Midsummer Night's Dream', its
poetry, its mix – the grand human Court of
Theseus and Hippolyta mirrored by the fairy
Court of Oberon and Titania; the passionate
silliness of the Athenian lovers ('Lord, what
fools these mortals be!' Puck gloats, but is
anyone sillier than his Fairy Queen?); and the
glorious comic underpinning of it all by
the mechanicals.*

*But Puck in this show? Heartless like all
hobgoblins, and at the best androgynous, Puck
doesn't fill the brief . . . so from 'The Dream'
I've chosen Hermia. She is not accounted one
of Shakespeare's great ladies, but she's a
faithful and fiery lover.*

*Puck has laid magic juice on the wrong lover's
eyes and the waking Lysander, who has wooed
Hermia, becomes infatuated with 'the first
live thing' he sees – her schoolfriend Helena.
On this bewitched and bewildering midsummer
night, Hermia, victim of love turned awry,
confronts her 'cheating' sweetheart and her
'cheating' friend . . .*

HERMIA

Why are you grown so rude, what change is this?
Sweet love, do you not jest? . . . What!
Can you do me greater harm than hate?
Hate me? Wherefore? O me! What news, my love?
Am I not Hermia? Are you not Lysander?
I am as fair now as I was erewhile.
Since night you lov'd me; yet since night you left me:
Why then you left me – O, the gods forbid!
In earnest shall I say?   (*To Helena.*)
O me! you juggler! you canker-blossom! You . . .
Thief of love! what! have you come by night
And stol'n my love's heart from him?
'Puppet'! why, so: ay, that way goes the game.
Now I perceive that she hath made compare
Between our statures: she hath urg'd her height;
And with her personage, her tall personage,
Her height forsooth, she hath prevail'd with him.
And are you grown so high in his esteem,
Because I am so dwarfish, and so low?
How low am I, thou painted maypole? Speak!
How low am I? I am not yet so low
But that my nails can reach unto thine eyes.

A Midsummer Night's Dream, Act III, Scene 2

Measure for Measure
The Merchant of Venice

I have yoked Isabella in 'Measure for Measure' to Portia in 'The Merchant of Venice' as two slants on the nature of mercy.

Isabella, a novice nun, pleads for her brother's life. He has impregnated his fiancée, and in the Duke's absence the local laws of morality are being reinforced by his deputy, the puritanical Angelo.

On tour recently in Hartlepool (like all resorts, sad out of season) on a lowering day in Spring I watched grey-green, rain-slashed seas through my big bay B&B window and re-read 'Measure for Measure' – and found myself quite suddenly shivering with joy and pleasure, real transports of joy! This scene particularly thrilled me, feeling Isabella evolve from unhopeful suitor – to engaged appellant – to passionate petitioner. Questions, intuitions, philosophy tumble out of her, as her plea for her brother reaches out to embrace all humanity while deputy Angelo argues, lusting as much after her rigorous soul as her beauty.

Portia's appeal to Shylock is no less passionate. She too, has a personal motive when she pleads, cross-dressed as a lawyer, for her husband's friend – but this appeal has a loftiness aimed more at the head than the heart. Mercy has become an abstract ideal. Portia invokes the present, the human, only when she gives reason to 'render the deeds of mercy'.

I am a woeful suitor to your honour
Please but your honour hear me.
I have a brother is condemned to die,
I do beseech you, let it be his fault
And not my brother. Must he needs die?
I do think that you might pardon him
And neither heaven nor man grieve at the mercy.
Too late? Why, no; I that do speak a word
May call it back again. Well believe this,
No ceremony that to great ones 'longs
Not the king's crown, nor the deputed sword,
The marshal's truncheon, nor the judge's robe
Become them with one half so good a grace
As mercy does. Alas, alas!
Why, all the souls that were were forfeit once,
And He that might the vantage best have took,
Found out the remedy. How would you be,
If He, which is the top of judgement, should
But judge you, as you are? O, think on that
And mercy then will breathe within your lips,
Like man new made. – Tomorrow!
O, that's sudden. Spare him, spare him!
He's not prepared for death.
Good, good my lord, bethink you:
Who is it that hath died for this offence?
There's many have committed it.
Yet show some pity! O, it is excellent
To have a giant's strength; but it is tyrannous
To use it like a giant. Could great men thunder
As Jove himself does, Jove would ne'er be quiet,
For every pelting, petty officer

Would use his heaven for thunder; nothing but
    thunder.
Merciful heaven!
Thou rather with thy sharp and sulphurous bolt
Split'st the unwedgeable and gnarled oak
Than the soft myrtle; but man, proud man,
Dressed in a little brief authority,
Most ignorant of what he's most assur'd
His glassy essence, like an angry ape,
Plays such fantastic tricks before high heaven
As make the angels weep . . .
Go to your bosom;
Knock there, and ask your heart what it doth know
That's like my brother's fault: if it confess
A natural guiltiness such as is his,
Let it not sound a thought upon your tongue
Against my brother's life. – Gentle, my lord, turn back!

Measure for Measure, Act II, Scene 2

PORTIA

Then must the Jew be merciful.
The quality of mercy is not strained,
It droppeth as the gentle rain from heaven
Upon the place beneath. It is twice blessed:
It blesseth him that gives and him that takes,
'Tis mightiest in the mightiest, it becomes
The throned monarch better than his crown.
His sceptre shows the force of temporal power,
The attribute to awe and majesty,
Wherein doth sit the dread and fear of kings:

But mercy is above this sceptred sway,
It is enthroned in the hearts of kings,
It is an attribute to God himself;
And earthly power doth then show likest God's,
When mercy seasons justice. Therefore, Jew,
Though justice be thy plea, consider this,
That in the course of justice none of us
Should see salvation: we do pray for mercy,
And that same prayer doth teach us all to render
The deeds of mercy.

The Merchant of Venice, Act IV, Scene 1

As You Like It

Cross-dressing in Illyria, in Venice, in the Forest of Arden . . . with the added piquancy of knowing that the first cross-dressing heroines were played by youths.

Four hundred years later the frequency of the device teases. Does it reflect Shakespeare's view of women's position in society?

If he had a view, don't we find it in the fact that he employs the device so often, using it to reveal – with his unique kind of psychological bi-sexuality – the world he lived in? Viola, Rosalind, Imogen in 'Cymbeline', Julia in 'Two Gentlemen of Verona' dress as men for protection, Portia for enablement because only as a 'justice', as a man, will she be listened to. Shakespeare shows that to be safe or heeded in his world, that's what you have to do – be a man if you're a woman, like his sovereign Elizabeth whose 'body of a weak and feeble woman' housed 'the heart and stomach of a king'.

'As You Like It' was the first Shakespeare play I saw, in a country rep as a schoolgirl. We all got crushes on the Orlando, an unknown actor called Nigel Hawthorne . . . Many years later we were to share a stage.

Rosalind is a favourite of mine, my second role at RADA. A duke's daughter in love with

Orlando, she is banished to the Forest of Arden
where she is accompanied by her cousin, the
usurping duke's daughter. And there, since she
is 'more than common tall', she cross-dresses as
a shepherd-boy to protect both herself and Celia.

In a forest glade Rosalind overhears Phebe, a
real shepherdess, rejecting her fiercely-pursuing
swain Silvius.

PHEBE

I would not be thy executioner!
I fly thee, for I would not injure thee.
Thou tell'st me there is murder in mine eye
'Tis pretty, sure, and very probable
That eyes, that are the frail'st and softest things,
Who shut their coward gates on atomies,
Should be call'd tyrants, butchers, murderers!
Now I do frown on thee with all my heart
And if mine eyes can wound, now let them kill thee!

Silvius sadly warns that one day she, too, may feel

'The wounds invisible that love's keen arrows make'

PHEBE

– But till that time
Come not thou near me; and when that time comes
Afflict me with thy mocks, pity me not,
As till that time I shall not pity thee.

Makes to exit, returning as Rosalind

And why, I pray you? Who might be your mother
That you insult, exult, and all at once
Over the wretched? What though you have no
    beauty –
As by my faith, I see no more in you
Than without candle may go dark to bed –
Must you therefore be proud and pitiless?
Why, what means this? Why do you look on me?
I see no more in you than in the ordinary
Of nature's sale-work. 'Od's my little life!
I think she means to tangle mine eyes too.
No, faith, proud mistress, hope not after it:
'Tis not your inky brows, your black silk hair
Your bugle eyeballs nor your cheeks of cream
That can entame my spirits to your worship!
You foolish shepherd, wherefore do you follow her,
Like foggy south, puffing with wind and rain?
You are a thousand times a properer man
Than she a woman! – But mistress,
Know thyself: down on your knees
And thank heaven, fasting, for a good man's love,
For I must tell you friendly in your ear,
Sell when you can; you are not for all markets.
So take her to thee, shepherd! Fare you well.

Makes to exit, returning as Phebe

PHEBE

'Whoever lov'd that lov'd not at first sight?' . . .
Know'st thou the youth that spoke to me erewhile?
Think not I love him, though I ask for him.
'Tis but a peevish boy; yet he talks well

But what care I for words? Yet words do well
When he that speaks them pleases those that hear.
It is a pretty youth: not very pretty:
But sure he's proud; and yet his pride becomes him;
He'll make a proper man: the best thing in him
Is his complexion; and faster than his tongue
Did make offence his eye did heal it up.
He's not very tall: but for his years he's tall
His leg is but so-so . . . and yet, 'tis well . . .
There be some women, Silvius, had they mark'd him
In parcels as I did, would have gone near
To fall in love with him; but for my part,
I love him not nor hate him not; and yet
Have more cause to hate him than to love him:
For what had he to do to chide at me?
He said mine eyes were black and my hair black
And now I am remember'd, scorn'd at me.
I marvel why I answer'd not again!
But that's all one; omittance is no quittance.
I'll write to him a very taunting letter
And thou shalt bear it: wilt thou, Silvius?

As You Like It, Act III, Scene 5

Troilus and Cressida

Poor Phebe, briefly felled by misplaced love . . .

*And now Cressida, and the love that will
betray . . . in the city of Troy, nearly three
thousand years ago.*

*Troy has been under siege to the Greeks for
ten years. Inside the city Troilus and Cressida
make their first shy admissions of love. Troilus
swears his name will become a yardstick for
'truth' – 'as true as Troilus' – prompting a
reply whose bitter irony will in hindsight ring
through the ages.*

*For Cressida, whose father has already defected
to the Greeks, will be sent by her townsmen to
the Greek camp as barter for their local heroes.
Flattered and fêted there by the soldiers she,
too, will betray her Trojan origins – and her
lover Troilus.*

*In the heady first days of their love-affair,
Troilus asks why she was so hard to win.*

Hard to seem won; but I was won, my lord
With the first glance that ever – pardon me;
If I confess much you will play the tyrant.
I love you now; but not, till now, so much
But I might master it. In faith, I lie!
My thoughts were like unbridled children grown
Too headstrong for their mother. See, we fools!
Why have I blabbed? Who shall be true to us
When we are so unsecret to ourselves?
But though I loved you well, I wooed you not;
And yet, good faith, I wished myself a man,
Or that we women had men's privilege
Of speaking first. Sweet, bid me hold my tongue!
For in this rapture I shall surely speak
The thing I shall repent. See, see, your silence,
Cunning in dumbness, from my weakness draws
My very soul of counsel! Stop my mouth.
– My lord, I do beseech you, pardon me:
'Twas not my purpose thus to beg a kiss.
I am ashamed. Oh heavens, what have I done?
. . . I have a kind of self resides with you,
But an unkind self that itself will leave
To be another's fool. I would be gone.
If I be false, or swerve a hair from truth,
When time is old and hath forgot itself,
When waterdrops have worn the stones of Troy,
And blind oblivion swallowed cities up,
And mighty states characterless are grated
To dusty nothing, yet let memory
From false to false, among false maids in love
Upbraid my falsehood! When they've said 'as false

As air, as water, wind or sandy earth,
As fox to lamb, or wolf to heifer's calf,
Pard to the hind, or stepdame to her son' –
Yea, let them say to stick the heart of falsehood,
'As false as Cressid'.

Troilus and Cressida, Act III, Scene 2

'Slut!' I was dismayed by this off-hand dismissal
of Cressida as a slut, as if that were all she'd
ever been – for isn't it just her youthful,
passionate sincerity that leaves the after-taste
more bitter? Isn't that what makes her resonate
through the centuries?

A playful, nimble-witted innocent in those
early scenes, she's far more human than the
satirised heroes she's amongst – and it's that
lost innocence you mourn when, a victim of
war fighting her corner, she betrays Troilius.
You watch her at those crossroads . . . live
her dilemma . . . and when it's all over, you're
left with that heart-in-mouth feeling 'There but
for the grace of God . . . ' she resonates.

Much Ado about Nothing
The Taming of the Shrew

*Another nimble woman – of another age,
another culture is Beatrice in 'Much Ado About
Nothing', an only child who terrifies men with
her enamelled wit.*

*Like Katharina the Shrew who terrorises with
her temper, Beatrice has lacked a mother from
an early age. These feisty young women would
see themselves as anti-romantics, but 'the lady
doth protest too much' perhaps; it's genuine
fear – of men per se, a loss of autonomy, or
simply the giving of self? – that underscores
them both. Kate and Beatrice will have to be
tricked into love, and like all real heroes,
they're capable of change.*

*First Katharina of Padua, the sister who feels
less loved of her father and who punishes the
world for her perceived unloveliness – father,
sister, suitors, herself – with tantrums, fists
and fights. And there she would stew in her
own unhappy juice were it not for the wooing
of the still rougher, but finally as seduced-
as-seducing, dowry-hunter Petruccio. The
moment when Kate loved becomes Kate
loving (if not forever obedient) has yet to
come. Now she honeymoons on a regime of
brawls and famine.*

The more my wrong, the more his spite appears
What, did he marry me to famish me?
Beggars that come unto my father's door
Upon entreaty have a present alms;
If not, elsewhere they meet with charity:
But I, who never knew how to entreat,
Nor never needed that I should entreat,
Am starv'd for meat, giddy for lack of sleep;
With oaths kept waking, and with brawling fed,
And that which spites me more than all these wants,
He does it under name of perfect love;
As who should say, if I should sleep or eat
'Twere deadly sickness, or else present death.
I prithee, go and get me some repast:
I care not what, so it be wholesome food.
'How say you to a fat tripe nicely broil'd?'
I like it well: good Grumio, fetch it me.
'What say you to a piece of beef and mustard?'
A dish that I do love to feed upon!
Or then the beef, and let the mustard rest,
Or both, or one, or anything thou wilt!
Go, get thee gone, thou false deluding slave
That feeds me with the very name of meat
Sorrow on thee, and all the pack of you
That triumph thus upon my misery!
Go, get you gone I say.

The Taming of the Shrew, Act IV, Scene 3

*In 'Much Ado' Beatrice's dazzle of language
protects her from the delights and pains of love
till she meets her match in Benedick. Their
battle of wits becomes as fierce as Kate and
Petruccio's rough-house – and only the
physicality of a kiss will breach the wall of
words between.*

*In this early scene Beatrice airs her views on
marriage.*

BEATRICE

How tartly that gentleman looks. I never can see
him but I am heart-burned an hour after. He were
an excellent man that were made just in the mid-
way between him and Benedick. The one is too like
an image and says nothing, and the other too like
my lady's eldest son, evermore tattling. With a good
leg and a good foot, uncle, and money enough in
his purse, such a man would win any woman in the
world if 'a could get her goodwill.

. . . Too curst is more than curst. I shall lessen
God's sending that way, for it is said 'God sends a
curst cow short horns' – but to a cow too curst he
sends none. Just! if he send me no husband, for the
which blessing I am at him, upon my knees, every
morning and evening! Lord, I could not endure a
husband with a beard on his face – I had rather lie
in the woollen! And a husband that hath no beard –
what should I do with him? Dress him in my
apparel and make him my waiting-woman?

He that hath a beard is more than a youth, and he that hath no beard is less than a man; and he that is more than a youth is not for me, and he that is less than a man, I am not for him. Therefore I will even take sixpence, and lead these apes into hell! To the gate, and there will the devil meet me like an old cuckold with horns on his head, and say 'Get you to heaven, Beatrice, get you to heaven – here's no place for you maids.'

So deliver I up my apes, and away to St Peter: for the heavens he shows me where the bachelors sit, and there live we as merry as the day is long.

Much Ado About Nothing, Act II, Scene 1

To me, fair friend, you never can be old,
For as you were when first your eye I ey'd,
Such seems your beauty still. Three winters cold
Have from the forests shook three summers' pride,
Three beauteous springs to yellow autumn turn'd
In process of the seasons have I seen,
Three April perfumes in three hot Junes burn'd,
Since first I saw you fresh, which yet are green.
Ah! Yet doth beauty, like a dial hand,
Steal from his figure, and no pace perceiv'd:
So your sweet hue, which methinks still doth stand,
Hath motion, and mine eye may be deceiv'd;
   For fear of which, hear this, thou age unbred:
   Ere you were born was beauty's summer dead.

PART TWO

Mid Years and Beyond

CLEOPATRA

I dream'd there was an Emperor Antony:
O! such another sleep, that I might see
But such another man.
His face was as the heavens, and therein stuck
A sun and moon, which kept their course and lighted
The little O, the earth.
His legs bestrid the ocean: his rear'd arm
Crested the world; his voice was propertied
As all the tuned spheres, and that to friends;
But when he meant to quail and shake the orb
He was as rattling thunder. For his bounty
There was no winter in't, an autumn 'twas
That grew the more by reaping; his delights
Were dolphin-like, they showed his back above
The element they lived in: in his livery
Walk'd crowns and crownets, realms and islands were
As plates dropp'd from his pocket
Think you there was, or might be such a man
As this I dream'd of?

Antony and Cleopatra, Act V, Scene 2

Antony and Cleopatra
Macbeth

Cleopatra, Queen of Egypt, whom Enobarbus watched 'hop forty paces through the public street' is a creature of 'infinite variety', wild, vain, excessive, and haunted by Death. Does she truly love Antony or is she using him to secure her own borders? Twice she deserts him in battle, then sends a false report of her death; but when Antony returns to die in her arms, neither she nor we can doubt the reality of her love.

Shakespeare wrote 'Macbeth' just before 'Antony'. Perhaps the same boy actor who was to give his Cleopatra had practised with the almost as complex, certainly as driven, Lady Macbeth.

When Macbeth sends word of the witches' prophesy: 'thou shalt be king hereafter!' Lady Macbeth calls upon the spirits to 'unsex' her. She re-directs her love and her formidable sexual energy into realising his ambition – goads him, mocks him, quells his imagination and his conscience, masterminds Duncan's murder; takes in effect the controlling, 'male' role, in the relationship.

The violence she sets off, Macbeth completes, until both are engulfed by it . . . love turned awry indeed.

Was the hope drunk
Wherein you dress'd yourself? Hath it slept since?
And wakes it now, to look so green and pale
At what it did so freely? From this time
Such I account thy love. Art thou afeard
To be the same in thine own act and valour
As thou art in desire? Wouldst thou have that
Which thou esteem'st the ornament of life,
And live a coward in thine own esteem,
Letting 'I dare not' wait upon 'I would'
Like the poor cat i' th' adage?
When you durst do it, then you were a man
And to be more than what you were, you would
Be so much more the man. Nor time nor place
Did then adhere, and yet you would make both:
They have made themselves, and that their fitness now
Does unmake you. I have given suck, and know
How tender 'tis to love the babe that milks me:
I would, while it was smiling in my face,
Have pluck'd my nipple from his boneless gums
And dash'd the brains out, had I so sworn as you
Have done to this. – If we should fail, we fail!
But screw your courage to the sticking place
And we'll not fail.

Macbeth, Act I, Scene 7

Hamlet

*From queen to would-be queen and on to
another queen, Gertrude: her elegy for
Ophelia, the daughter she never had.*

*For me it's very important not to judge a
character I play – if I do, I stay outside her.*

*I'd studied 'Hamlet' at my Scottish grammar
school. Aeons later at Stratford, Gertrude –
damned as 'silly and shallow like a sheep in
the sun' by my old schoolteacher, Gowdie –
proved elusive. Weeks into rehearsal and no
nearer her kernel, I suddenly realised that
Gertrude had no such view of herself,
remembered that as an actor you have to look
out at the world through your character's eyes
alone. And as I got to know her, worn like a
jewel on her first husband's finger, immured
since girlhood in that bleak, male-dominated
Danish Court, my sense of Gertrude's
loneliness was overwhelming, of the yearning
she must feel for female companionship, of her
love for Hamlet, the sun of her life – and of
her potential for love, her real longing for
closeness with the girl he might one day marry.*

*Shortly after the closet-scene in which Hamlet
arraigns his mother for her 'infidelity' and
accuses Claudius of murder, the shell-shocked
Gertrude tells Laertes of her lonely discovery
by the river.*

GERTRUDE

Your sister's drown'd, Laertes.
There is a willow grows aslant a brook
That shows his hoar leaves in the glassy stream;
Therewith fantastic garlands did she make
Of crowflowers, nettles, daisies and long purples
That liberal shepherds give a grosser name
But our cold maids do dead men's fingers call them.
There, on the pendent boughs her coronet weeds
Clamb'ring to hang, an envious sliver broke;
When down her weedy trophies and herself
Fell in the weeping brook. Her clothes spread wide
And, mermaid-like awhile they bore her up,
Which time she chanted snatches of old songs
As one incapable of her own distress,
Or like a creature native and endued
Unto that element; but long it could not be
Till that her garments heavy with their drink,
Pull'd the poor wretch from her melodious lay
To muddy death. Drown'd, drown'd!

Hamlet, Act IV, Scene 7

Henry V

A very different elegy. Mistress Quickly, droll and earthy keeper of a bawdy-house, mourns her comrade, the rumbustious knight John Falstaff.

In 'Henry IV' Falstaff had been given a lethal come-uppance. His beloved Hal – the prince who had received at Falstaff's hands if not his 'sentimental' at least his 'street' education, the education which would make of Hal that unheard of thing in a king, a man of the people – Hal is crowned. Then tells his eager mentor: 'I know thee not, old man' . . . Is there a briefer, more hope-defying rejection in literature?

Falstaff hears it and turns his face to the wall . . . but Elizabeth I turned it back. She commanded a second play about Falstaff, 'The Merry Wives of Windsor'.

What was it that both Shakespeare's sovereign and the young Hal himself so dearly loved in Falstaff? Why have audiences from the Elizabethans on, been so proud that he stands as a quintessential image of England? Braggart, blaggard, liar, lecher, coward, drunk, thief; but to describe someone as 'Falstaffian' is to conjure the image of a person with a gargantuan appetite for life – feckless,

generous, sinning, excessive, and with a child-
like trust in others that is dangerous and rare.

Here the questionable, but equally human
Mistress Quickly relates his end to their friends
at the Boar's Tavern.

MISTRESS QUICKLY

Nay, sure, he's not in hell, he's in Arthur's bosom, if
ever man went to Arthur's bosom. 'A made a finer
end, and went away an it had been any christom
child; 'a parted ev'n just between twelve and one,
ev'n at the turning o' th' tide; for after I saw him
fumble with the sheets and play with flowers, and
smile upon his finger's end, I knew there was but
one way for his nose was as sharp as a pen and 'a
babbled of green fields . . . . 'How now, Sir John!'
quoth I. 'What, man, be of good cheer'. So 'a cried
out 'God, God, God!' three or four times.

Now I, to comfort him, bid him 'a should not think
of God: I hop'd there was no need to trouble Him
with any such thoughts as yet . . . So 'a bade me lay
more clothes on his feet; I put my hand into the bed
and felt them, and they were as cold as any stone;
then I felt to his knees, and so up'ard and up'ard,
and all was as cold as any stone.

Cried out of sack, they say? Ay, that 'a did. And
of women? Nay, that 'a did not. 'A said they were
devils incarnate. 'A never could abide carnation;
'twas a colour 'a never liked . . . . 'A did in some

sort, indeed, handle women; but then 'a was rheumatic, and talked of the whore of Babylon. Do you not remember 'a saw a flea stick upon Bardolph's nose, and 'a said it was a black soul burning in hell-fire? Well, the fuel's gone that maintain'd that fire.

Henry V, Act II, Scene 3

Othello

*In 'Othello', while Iago subtly persuades the
Moor of Desdemona's infidelity, Emilia remains
strangely blind to her husband's capacity for
evil. For worldly as she is, Emilia has an innate
kind of innocence which recognises the same
quality in its pristine state in her mistress.*

*When she discovers the dead Desdemona –
Othello as murderer: Iago as villain – her love
for her mistress is re-inforced by a passion for
truth. This two-fold love forbids Emilia to be
silent, and she will die for it.*

EMILIA

Out and alas! that was my lady's voice
O lady, speak again! Sweet Desdemona!
O sweet mistress, speak!
Who hath done this deed? 'Twas you that kill'd her.
O, the more angel she, and you the blacker devil!
Thou'rt rash as fire to say that she was false
O, she was heavenly true!
                              My husband?
My husband knew it all? That she was false to wedlock?
If he say so, may his pernicious soul
Rot half a grain a day. He lies to the heart.
She was too fond of her most filthy bargain!
Ha, do thy worst. Thou hast not half that power
To do me harm as I have to be hurt.

O gull! O dolt! I care not for thy sword;
I'll make thee known though I lost twenty lives.
So, are you come, Iago? You have done well
That men must lay their murders on your neck.
Disprove this villain if thou be'st a man:
He says you told him that his wife was false
I know thou didst not: thou art not such a villain
Speak, for my heart is full
You told a lie! an odious damned lie!
Upon my soul, a lie – a wicked lie.
She, false with Cassio! Did you say with Cassio?
Good gentlemen, let me have leave to speak
'Tis proper I obey him, but not now.
Perchance Iago, I will ne'er go home. (*To Othello.*)
Nay, lay thee down and roar;
For thou hast kill'd the sweetest innocent
That e'er did lift up eye. 'Twill out,
'Twill out. – I, peace! No,
I will speak as liberal as the north,
Let heaven and men and devils, let them all
All, all, cry shame against me, yet I'll speak.
O thou dull Moor! That handkerchief thou speak'st of
I found by fortune, and did give my husband.
She give it Cassio! No, alas, I found it,
And I did give't my husband. By heaven I do not lie,
I do not, gentlemen! O murderous coxcomb!
What should such a fool do, with so good a wife?

Iago stabs her

Ay, ay. O lay me by my mistress' side.
What did thy song bode, lady? Hark . . .
Canst thou hear me? I will play the swan,
And die in music. (*Sings*.) 'Willow, willow, willow . . . '

Othello, Act V, Scene 2

Sonnet CXVI
Henry VIII

*This next needs no explaining, it's a sonnet for
all of us at our ideal best . . . and I think might
also stand as Katharine of Aragon's silent
testament of faith when, after twenty happy
years of marriage, she addresses Henry VIII
before Cardinal Wolsey to defend her title as
his wife.*

*The King is seeking an annulment so that he
can marry the youthful Anne Boleyn, for Anne
might produce strong sons. Instead she will
produce history's strongest queen,
Shakespeare's sovereign, Elizabeth I of
England.*

What Katharine might *have said to Henry,
then . . . and what she did.*

SONNET CXVI

Let me not to the marriage of true minds
Admit impediments. Love is not love
Which alters when it alteration finds,
Or bends with the remover to remove:
O, no! it is an ever-fixed mark,
That looks on tempests and is never shaken;
It is the star to every wandering barque,
Whose worth's unknown, although his height
    be taken.
Love's not Time's fool, though rosy lips and cheeks
Within his bending sickle's compass come:
Love alters not with his brief hours and weeks,
But bears it out even to the edge of doom.
        If this be error and upon me prov'd
        I never writ, nor no man ever lov'd.

QUEEN KATHARINE

Sir, I desire you do me right and justice;
And to bestow your pity on me: for
I am a most poor woman, and a stranger
Born out of your dominions; having here
No judge indifferent, nor no more assurance
Of equal friendship and proceeding. Alas, sir!
In what have I offended you? What cause
Hath my behaviour given to your displeasure,
That thus you should proceed to put me off
And take your good grace from me? Heaven witness,
I have been to you a true and humble wife,
At all times to your will conformable;

Ever in fear to kindle your dislike,
Yea, subject to your countenance, glad or sorry
As I saw it inclin'd. When was the hour
I ever contradicted your desire,
Or made it not mine too? Or which of your friends
Have I not strove to love, although I knew
He were mine enemy? What friend of mine
That had to him deriv'd your anger, did I
Continue in my liking? Nay, gave notice
He was from then discharg'd. Sir, call to mind
That I have been your wife in this obedience
Upward of twenty years, and have been blest
With many children by you; if in the course
And process of this time, you can report
And prove it too, against mine honour aught,
My bond to wedlock, or my love and duty
Against your sacred person, in God's name
Turn me away; and let the foul'st contempt
Shut door upon me, and so give me up
To the sharp'st kind of justice.
Your pleasure be fulfill'd!

Henry VIII, Act II, Scene 4

The Merry Wives of Windsor

*Very different wives, the 'merry' ones, Mistresses
Page and Ford – wealthy, fun-loving English
burghers. At their hands the gargantuan knight
John Falstaff – resurrected by royal command –
will be stuck in a basket of dirty washing,
tipped in the river, disguised as a washer-
woman to escape a jealous husband, and
finally set up as laughing-stock of Windsor.*

*Impecunious as ever, Falstaff woos them in
identical terms, two letters where only the
names are different, in the happy hope that one
or other will fall from her well-cushioned
perch, succumb to his charms and produce the
purse. Both are thrilled to receive a love-letter,
then mortified to discover its unprepossessing
source. Meg Page, practical, maternal,
comfortably married, is a superb conspirator,
but it is the more vulnerably-married Alice
Ford, the 'sexy', and apparently sillier wife,
who initiates the japes. She makes assignations
with Falstaff, then pulls the rug from under his
feet; and manages along the way to teach not
only Falstaff but her overweeningly jealous
husband a lesson – to trust in love.*

*I recently played Alice for the Royal
Shakespeare Company, with Joanna McCallum
as my fellow wife. Without Jo, alas! Here are
Meg Page and Alice Ford as they react to
Falstaff's letters . . .*

What! have I 'scaped love-letters in the holiday time
of my beauty, and am I now a subject for them? Let
me see:

'Ask me no reason why I love you; for though Love
use Reason for his physician, he admits him not for
his counsellor. You are not young, no more am I; go
to, there's sympathy; you are merry, so am I; ha! ha!
there's more sympathy: you love sack, and so do I –
would you desire better sympathy? Let it suffice
thee, Mistress Page, at the least, if the love of a
soldier can suffice, that I love thee. I will not say
'pity me' – 'tis not a soldier-like phrase; but I say
'love me'.

> By me,
> Thine own true knight,
> By day or night,
> Or any kind of light,
> With all his might
> For thee to fight,
>   JOHN FALSTAFF.'

O wicked, wicked world! One that is well-nigh
worn to pieces with age, to show himself the young
gallant! What an unweigh'd behaviour hath this
Flemish drunkard picked with the devil's name! out
of my conversation, that he dares in this manner
assay me? Why, he hath not been thrice in my
company – what did I say to him? I was then frugal
of my mirth, heaven forgive me! Why, I'll exhibit
a bill in the parliament for the putting down of

men. How shall I be revenged on him? For revenged I will be, as sure as his guts are made of puddings!

Makes to exit, returning as Mistress Ford

MISTRESS FORD

Mistress Page, Mistress Page! Trust me, I was coming to your house! O Mistress Page, give me some counsel! O woman, if it were not for one trifling respect, I could be knighted – Sir Alice Ford! We burn daylight. Here, read, read; perceive how I might be knighted . . . I shall think the worse of fat men as long as I have an eye to make difference of men's liking. And yet he would not swear; praised women's modesty; and gave such orderly and well-behaved reproof to all uncomeliness that I would have sworn his disposition would have gone to the truth of his words: but they do no more adhere and keep place together than the Hundredth Psalm to the tune of 'Greensleeves'! What tempest, I trow, threw this whale with so many tuns of oil in his belly ashore at Windsor? How shall I be revenged on him? I think the best way were to entertain him with hope, till the wicked fire of lust hath melted him in his own grease.

Did you ever read the like? (*Seeing Mistress Page's letter.*) Why, 'tis the very same! The very hand, the very words!

The Merry Wives of Windsor, Act II, Scene 1

Henry VI, Part III

If that was a hymn to fun, this is a hymn of hate. It's said that love and hate are two sides of the same coin, and the most passionate lovers are often the fiercest haters. Such a creature of extremes is Margaret – wife of Henry VI of Lancaster; long-term mistress of the Earl of Suffolk, and mother of Edward, heir to the English throne.

Margaret is introduced as the teen-age Princess of Anjou in the 'Henry VI' trilogy, when she is wooed by the besotted Suffolk for his king.

Over the next three or four decades as Queen of England, she takes the 'male' role in her marriage, dominating Henry and the turbulent country she has married into. For England is riven by war, the dynastic Wars of the Roses, the white rose of York warring with the red rose of Lancaster in dispute of Henry's claim.

The 'she-wolf of France' becomes more patriotic, more English as the years roll on. She survives the despair of her lover Suffolk's execution, plots and connives in Lancastrian interests – but when Henry agrees to disinherit their son at his death in favour of York, she, like England, is riven.

Riven by love, riven by hate: by love for the son whose inheritance is lost, by love for her adopted country, by an angry, protective love

*for Henry – and by a deadly hatred for the
usurping York, whose own sons will prove her
nemesis.*

*Briefly victorious on the battlefield she
confronts her enemy.*

QUEEN MARGARET

Brave warriors, Clifford and Northumberland,
Come, make him stand upon this molehill here
That wrought at mountains with outstretched arms
Yet parted but the shadow with his hand.
What! Was it you that would be England's king?
Was't you that revell'd in our Parliament,
And made a preachment of your high descent?
Where are your mess of sons to back you now?
The wanton Edward, and the lusty George?
And where's that valiant crookback prodigy,
Dicky your boy, that with his grumbling voice
Was wont to cheer his dad in mutinies?
Or, with the rest, where is your darling Rutland?
Look, York: I stain'd this napkin with the blood
That valiant Clifford with his rapier's point
Made issue from the bosom of thy boy;
I give thee this to dry thy cheeks withal.
What! hath thy fiery heart so parch'd thine entrails
That not a tear can fall for Rutland's death?
Why art thou patient, man? Thou shouldst be mad;
And I to make thee mad, do mock thee thus.
Stamp, rave, and fret that I may sing and dance.
York cannot speak unless he wears a crown!
A crown for York! And lords, bow low to him:

Hold you his hands whilst I do set it on.
Ay, marry, sir, now looks he like a king!
Ay, this is he that took King Henry's chair;
And this is he was his adopted heir.
But how is it that great Plantagenet
Is crown'd so soon, and broke his solemn oath?
As I bethink me, you should not be king
Till our King Henry had shook hands with death.
And will you pale your head in Henry's glory,
And rob his temples of the diadem
Now in his life, against your holy oath?
O! 'tis a fault too, too unpardonable.
Off with the crown; and with the crown, his head;
And whilst we breathe, take time to do him dead.

Henry VI, Part 3, Act I, Scene 4

King John

*This lament of Constance for her young son
Arthur is timeless, placeless. Every day in
Palestine, Rwanda, Chechinya, the Balkans, a
mother weeps for her child.*

*It's 1202, three years before England's Magna
Carta which for the first time challenged the
'divine right of kings'. Prince Arthur is rightful
heir to the throne but has been usurped by his
uncle, King John the first – and last, so bad
there wasn't a second.*

*The barons are restless, but irresolute.
Constance has enlisted support for Arthur's
cause from the French Philip II, who demands
John's abdication. War between France and
England flares again, and when the two armies
meet at Angers, Constance and Arthur fight
against their own countrymen. But the French
have been routed, the young Arthur captured
and returned to England – there to be
incarcerated by John, then blinded and
murdered.*

*Stranded in France, Constance agonises to the
king and his cardinal.*

Thou sayst I utter 'madness and not sorrow';
Thou art not holy to belie me so.
I am not mad; this hair I tear is mine;
My name is Constance; I was Geoffrey's wife;
Young Arthur is my son, and he is lost!
I am not mad: I would to heaven I were!
For then 'tis like I should forget myself
O! if I could, what grief should I forget!
Preach some philosophy to make me mad,
And thou shalt be canonis'd, cardinal;
For being not mad but sensible of grief,
My reasonable part produces reason
How I may be delivered of these woes,
And teaches me to kill or hang myself:
If I were mad, I should forget my son,
Or madly think a babe of clouts were he.
I am not mad: too well, too well I feel
The different plague of each calamity!
There was not such a gracious creature born.
But now will canker-sorrow eat my bud
And chase the native beauty from his cheek,
And he will look as hollow as a ghost,
As dim and meagre as an ague's fit,
And so he'll die; and rising so again
When I shall meet him in the court of heaven
I shall not know him: therefore never, never
Must I behold my pretty Arthur more.
'As fond of grief' you say, 'as of my child'
He talks to me that never had a son.
Grief fills the room up of my absent child,

Lies in his bed, walks up and down with me,
Puts on his pretty looks, repeats his words,
Remembers me of all his gracious parts,
Stuffs out his vacant garments with his form:
Then have I reason to be fond of grief.
O Lord! my boy, my Arthur, my fair son!
My life, my joy, my food, my all the world!

King John, Act III, Scene 4

Shakespeare in My Life

I became entranced as a child, growing up on the west coast of Scotland, when, on a day too wet to go riding or rambling, some of his marvellous men and women walked out of the dark-green, leather-bound volumes amongst my actor-manqué stepfather's bookshelves.

There was Shakespeare in school, then at RADA . . . then somehow I lost him; did film, theatre, television work all over the globe, almost no classical work. Until one summer in Connecticut and a production of 'Hamlet' between a duckpond and a railway-line, when the Prince of Denmark's tragedy unfolded to the rattle of family picnics below on the grass, thunder of trains (long ones every quarter-of-an-hour) behind, and a good deal of smothered giggling by the actors which rose to a crescendo as stars came out and our audience melted away.

I'd been hooked once more. Back in England I joined the Royal Shakespeare Company, and fell properly in love all over again.

When calls came to drop the 'Man of the Millennium' from the state school curriculum, I was off on a quest . . . unsure of arriving, but wanting to share the journey.

O! never say that I was false of heart,
Though absence seem'd my flame to qualify.
As easy might I from myself depart
As from my soul, which in thy breast doth lie:
This is my home of love: if I have rang'd,
Like him that travels, I return again;
Just to the time, not with the time exchang'd,
So that myself bring water for my stain.
Never believe, though in my nature reign'd
All frailties that beseige all kinds of blood,
That it could so preposterously be stain'd
To leave for nothing all thy sum of good;
    For nothing this wide universe I call,
      Save thou, my rose, in it thou art my all.

Epilogue

It is not the fashion to see the lady the epilogue;
but it is no more unhandsome than to see the lord
the prologue. If it be true that good wine needs no
bush, 'tis true that a good play needs no epilogue;
yet to good wine, they do use good bushes, and
good plays prove the better by the help of good
epilogues. What a case am I in then, that am neither
a good epilogue nor cannot insinuate with you in
the behalf of a good play!

I am not furnished like a beggar, therefore to beg
will not become me: my way is to conjure you;
and I'll begin with the women. I charge you,
O women! to like as much of this play as please
you: and I charge you, O men! for the love you
bear to women – as I perceive by your simpering,
none of you hate them – that between you and the
women, the play may please. If I were a woman,
I would kiss as many of you as have beards that
pleased me, complexions that liked me, and breaths
that I defied not: and I am sure as many as have
good beards, or good faces, or sweet breaths, will
for my kind offer when I make curtsy, bid me
farewell.

As You Like It

POSSIBLES
and
POSSIBILITIES

*Give or take the odd memory/reflection that
creeps willy-nilly into 'link' passages, the show
runs something short of two hours. But after
my Georgian experience and then at the
American school in Budapest, I felt a real
urgency to create a version which would last
an hour without interval, a show I could tour
where English is not widely spoken, or take to
schools and colleges.*

*Then someone who'd seen the first 'work-in-
progress' invited me to sing for my New Year
supper at a Venetian masked ball. In a
beautiful Renaissance palazzo, would I
contribute 'twenty minutes or so' towards an
evening where music from a string quartet
would intersperse with arias sung by two great
singers? All money raised would go towards
saving Venice from sinking into the sea.*

*And then I was approached by a fellow
festival-goer to Tibilisi. My grand patroness,
Keti Dolidze, who founded the International
White Scarf movement leading two thousand
women through the front line of Chechinya's
civil war, was coming to England to raise funds
for her country's drama students. Would I*

provide from my show a 'curtain-raiser' to her own one-woman play, which was to be staged at the Theatre Museum? . . . And the idea of presenting the show at the Edinburgh Festival arose – where, clearly, the scurry of Festival-time would hardly allow me an interval, and yet I be needn't be bound by the strict time-slot of an hour.

All this made me think how versatile 'The Loves of Shakespeare's Women' might be. The permutations began to seem endless as I re-imagined the show, then re-imagined again, sometimes in excitement, sometimes with sadness, for any one woman set aside felt like a small treachery.

The order of course, as well as the 'links' themselves, would have to change because whether in full version, short, or mini, I wanted to retain an internal structure and range, a sense of the variety of these women, as well as of their antitheses or their correspondences. And a mix besides, of comedy and drama, of 'ladies' and 'women', queens and commoners . . .

For the hour version, itself a 'work-in-progress' and as yet untried, I'd drop Katharina, Hermia, and probably Cressida among the younger women. Portia's speech on mercy is so well known that if pushed, I could drop that too (but I do like her! and coupling to Isabella). Of the older women I've tentatively set aside Gertrude, Lady Macbeth and Mistress Quickly, and since there'll be no interval, feel I could lose the bridge to them of Sonnet CIV.

So the hour version would run:

*When I was to sing for my supper in Venice
(which didn't happen), I planned to play
Viola, Beatrice, Cleopatra, and Constance –
and were more singing to be wanted, I'd
add Phebe/Rosalind, or Isabella; and Lady
Macbeth. I did, though, do the 'curtain-raiser'
for Keti Dolidze at the Theatre Museum. This
woman has been named one of the Hundred
Heroines of the World, and I wanted to honour
her courage as a war-heroine. Since the most
generous quality humans at war can exercise
must be mercy, I chose Isabella, Portia, and
learned one of my 'Possibles', Volumnia . . .
Doing this made me see how different
couplings, short 'blocks' of two or more of the
women could be created to illustrate one
aspect of love: women in love – Juliet, Viola,
Hermia, Imogen for example; parental and
'quasi-parental' love – Gertrude, Volumnia, the*

Countess of Roussillon, the Nurse in 'Romeo and Juliet'; cousin-love – Celia, and Beatrice's second speech; love betrayed or betraying – Helena in 'A Midsummer Night's Dream', Helena in 'All's Well That Ends Well', Cressida . . . and so on.

So what follows are a number of 'Possibles' I mentioned at the beginning of this book: characters I might one day interchange with some in the show. Among the young ones is the 'painted maypole', Helena, as an alternative to Hermia in 'The Dream'.

A Midsummer Night's Dream

Helena, formerly loved by Demetrius then spurned by him for Hermia, finds on this 'bewitched and bewildering midsummer night' both her former lover and Lysander – bewitched by Puck's mis-applied magic – vying for her favours. She supposes that they, with her old schoolfriend Hermia, have joined to mock her.

HELENA

O spite! O hell! I see you all are bent
To set against me for your merriment:
If you were civil and knew courtesy
You would not do me thus much injury.

Can you not hate me as I know you do,
But you must join in souls to mock me too?
If you were men, as men you are in show
You would not use a gentle lady so:
To vow, and swear, and superpraise my parts,
When I am sure you hate me with your hearts.
You both are rivals and love Hermia,
And now both rivals to mock Helena:
A trim exploit, a manly enterprise
To conjure tears up in a poor maid's eyes
With your derision! None of noble sort
Would so offend a virgin, and extort
A poor soul's patience, all to make you sport.
– Lo! She is one of this confederacy.
Now I perceive they have conjoin'd, all three,
To fashion this false sport in spite of me.
Injurious Hermia! Most ungrateful maid
Have you conspir'd, have you with these contriv'd
To bait me with this false derision?
Ay, do, persever, counterfeit sad looks,
Make mouths upon me when I turn my back;
Wink at each other; hold the sweet jest up:
If you have any pity, grace, or manners,
You would not make me such an argument.
But, fare ye well: 'tis partly mine own fault
Which death or absence soon will remedy.

Act III, Scene 2

All's Well that Ends Well

*Love that will be betrayed. Helena, an orphan
and ward of the Countess of Roussillon, is in
love with her 'foster' brother, the Countess's
son Bertram. Soon Helena will cure the King
of France of a potentially lethal illness and
claim in reward the unwilling Bertram's hand
in marriage – who will 'wed her, not bed her',
leave for the wars in Italy swearing not to
return until he 'have no wife' – then set about
wooing another.*

*But before all that, at the beginning of the play
Helena muses . . .*

HELENA

O! were that all. I think not on my father;
And these great tears grace his remembrance more
Than those I shed for him. What was he like?
I have forgot him: my imagination
Carries no favour in't but Bertram's.
I am undone: there is no living, none,
If Bertram be away. It were all one
That I should love a bright particular star
And think to wed it, he is so above me:
In his bright radiance and collateral light
Must I be comforted, not in his sphere.
The ambition in my love thus plagues itself:
The hind that would be mated by the lion
Must die for love. 'Twas pretty, though a plague,
To see him every hour; to sit and draw

His arched brows, his hawking eye, his curls,
In our heart's table; heart too capable
Of every line and trick of his sweet favour:
But now he's gone, and my idolatrous fancy
Must sanctify his relics.

Act I, Scene 1

Love's Labour's Lost

*King Ferdinand of Navarre has persuaded three
young nobles to join him in eschewing the
company of women, in favour of a three-year
period of study and contemplation. The
Princess of France arrives at court with her
three ladies-in-waiting. The four couples fall in
love, and the men decide to experiment with
their emotions and the ladies' – who prove
more than a match for them. Hi-jinks ensue,
involving games of wit, mistaken identities,
letters falling into wrong hands, drunkenness
and fights. At the height of the merrymaking,
an announcement comes of the King of
France's death. To Ferdinand's proposal of
marriage, the Princess replies . . .*

PRINCESS OF FRANCE

We have received your letters full of love;
Your favours, the ambassadors of love;
And in our maiden council, rated them
At courtship, pleasant jest, and courtesy,
As bombast and as lining to the time.

But more devout than this in our respects
Have we not been; and therefore met your loves
In their own fashion, like a merriment.
Now, at the latest minute of the hour,
To grant our loves –
   . . . a time methinks, too short
To make a world-without-end bargain in.
No, no, my lord, your Grace is perjur'd much,
Full of dear guiltiness: and therefore this:
If for my love, – as there is no such cause, –
You will do aught, this shall you do for me:
Your oath I will not trust; but go with speed
To some forlorn and naked hermitage,
Remote from all the pleasures of the world;
There stay, until the twelve celestial signs
Have brought about their annual reckoning.
If this austere, unsociable life
Change not your offer made in heat of blood;
If frosts and fasts, hard lodging and thin weeds
Nip not the gaudy blossoms of your love
But that it bear this trial and last love;
Then, at the expiration of the year,
Come challenge me, challenge me by these deserts
And, by this virgin palm now kissing thine,
I will be thine; and, till that instant, shut
My woeful self up in a mourning house,
For the remembrance of my father's death.
If this thou do deny, let our hands part;
Neither entitled in the other's heart.

Act V, Scene 2

Cymbeline

*Imogen, daughter of Cymbeline, King of
England, destined by her father to marry her
doltish stepbrother Cloten, has instead secretly
married Posthumus. He is banished to Rome,
setting sail from Milford Haven. Here Imogen
questions his servant Pisanio about Posthumus'
leave-taking.*

IMOGEN

I would thou grew'st unto the shores o' th' haven,
And questionedst every sail; if he should write
And I not have it, 'twere a paper lost
As offered mercy is. Thou shouldst have made him
As little as a crow, or less, ere left
To after-eye him.
I would have broke mine eye-strings, cracked
    them but
To look upon him, till the diminution
Of space had pointed him sharp as my needle,
Nay, followed him till he had melted from
The smallness of a gnat to air; and then
Have turned mine eye and wept.
. . . I did not take my leave of him, but had
Most pretty things to say. Ere I could tell him
How I would think on him at certain hours
Such thoughts and such; or I could make him swear
The shes of Italy should not betray
Mine interest and his honour; or have charged him,

At the sixth hour of morn, at noon, at midnight,
T' encounter me with orisons, for then
I am in heaven for him; or ere I could
Give him that parting kiss which I had set
Betwixt two charming words, comes in my father,
And like the tyrannous breathing of the north
Shakes all our buds from growing.

Act I, Scene 3

*Posthumus in Rome has boasted to Iachimo of
Imogen's fidelity, and Iachimo lays a bet that
he will seduce her. In England, hidden in a
trunk, he has himself smuggled into her
bedroom, observes her sleeping, steals her
bracelet, takes note of the furnishings, and
reports back in Rome that he has won his bet.
Posthumus instructs Pisanio to kill Imogen; but
the servant warns Imogen, who disguises
herself as a boy and escapes to Wales, where
she will be befriended by young shepherds . . .
For me, there is great charm and funniness here
in Imogen's bravado.*

IMOGEN

I see a man's life is a tedious one.
I have tired myself, and for two nights together
Have made the ground my bed. I should be sick
But that my resolution helps me. Milford,
When from the mountain-top Pisanio showed thee,
Thou wast within a ken. O Jove, I think
Foundations fly the wretched! Two beggars told me
I could not miss my way. Will poor fellows lie

That have afflictions on them, knowing 'tis
A punishment or trial? Yes, no wonder
When rich ones scarce tell true. To lapse in fullness
Is sorer than to lie for need; and falsehood
Is worse in kings than beggars. My dear lord,
Thou art one o' th' false ones. Now I think on thee
My hunger's gone; but even before, I was
At point to sink for food. But what is this?
Here is a path to't; 'tis some savage hold.
I were best not call; I dare not call; yet famine
Ere clean it o'erthrow nature, makes it valiant.
Plenty and peace breeds cowards; hardness ever
Of hardiness is mother. Ho! Who's here?
If anything that's civil, speak; if savage,
Take or lend. Ho! No answer? Then I'll enter.
Best draw my sword; and if mine enemy
But fear the sword like me, he'll scarcely look on't.
Such a foe, good heavens!

                                        Act III, Scene 6

Much Ado About Nothing

This is a marvellous alternative for Beatrice, an example of cousin-love that matches Celia's for Rosalind.

Beatrice and Benedick have confessed their love for each other, but Beatrice's cousin Hero, engaged to Claudio and falsely accused of consorting with another man, has been jilted and dishonoured by Claudio at the altar. At once Benedick seeks out Beatrice.

BEATRICE

You have stayed me in a happy hour; I was about to protest I loved you. I love you with so much of my heart that none is left to protest . . . Bid thee do anything for me?

Kill Claudio.

You kill me to deny it. Farewell . . . I am gone, though I am here; there is no love in you; nay, I pray you, let me go. In faith, I will go. You dare easier be friends with me than fight with mine enemy. – Is 'a not approved in the height a villain that hath slandered, scorned, dishonoured, my kinswoman? O that I were a man! What! Bear her in hand, until they come to take hands, and then with public accusation, uncover'd slander, unmitigated rancour – O God, that I were a man! I would eat his heart in the market-place. Talk with a man out at a

window! A proper saying! Sweet Hero! She is
wronged, she is slandered, she is undone. Princes
and Counties! Surely a princely testimony, a goodly
count, Count Comfit; a sweet gallant, surely! O that
I were a man for his sake! Or that I had any friend
would be a man for my sake! But manhood is
melted into courtesies, valour into compliment, and
men are only turned into tongue, and trim ones too.
He is now as valiant as Hercules that only tells a lie
and swears it. I cannot be a man with wishing,
therefore I will die a woman with grieving. The
Count Claudio hath wronged Hero as sure as I have
a thought or a soul.

Act IV, Scene 1

As You Like It

*Orlando, younger son of Sir Rowland de Boys,
has defeated Charles the Wrestler and won the
heart of Rosalind, niece of the usurping Duke
Frederick, and beloved cousin of Celia, the
Duke's daughter.*

*Jealous of her popularity with the people,
Duke Frederick banishes Rosalind from the
court, reminding Celia that her cousin had
received sanctuary as a child only so that she,
Celia, might have a playmate.*

I did not then entreat to have her stay:
It was your pleasure and your own remorse.
I was too young that time to value her;
But now I know her; if she be a traitor,
Why so am I. – Banish'd?
Pronounce that sentence then on me, my liege
I cannot live out of her company. *(Duke F. leaves)*
O my poor Rosalind! Whither wilt thou go?
Wilt thou change fathers? I will give thee mine.
Shall we be sund'red? Shall we part, sweet girl?
No, let my father seek another heir.
Therefore devise with me how we may fly,
Whither to go, and what to bear with us;
And do not seek to take your charge upon you,
To bear your griefs yourself and leave me out;
For by this heaven, now at our sorrows pale,
Say what thou canst, I'll go along with thee
To seek my uncle in the Forest of Arden.
I'll put myself in poor and mean attire
And with a kind of umber smirch my face;
The like do you; so shall we pass along,
And never stir assailants. Let's away
And get our jewels and our wealth together,
Devise the fittest time and safest way
To hide us from pursuit that will be made
After my flight. Now go we in content
To liberty, and not to banishment.

Act I, Scene 3

'In These Days' . . .

Those, then, are some young 'Possibles'.

Katharina's speech in Act V of 'The Taming
of the Shrew', beginning at 'A woman
mov'd is like a fountain troubled . . . '
could be a strong contender, but I decided
against it mainly because it's a-typical of
the Kate we know and love, and also
because in these days it's hard to receive
without a trace of delighted irony (and
harder still to deliver. I think I couldn't
manage it). Luciana's rebuke to Antipholus
of Syracuse when she mistakes him for her
brother-in-law in Act III, Scene 2 of 'The
Comedy of Errors' is a moving example of
sisterly love, and there are others, others . . .
I love the feeling that there are more to
delve for. And before I set down the older
'Possibles', I want to look at a question
also coloured by that 'in these days'.

Somebody asked me if I had anything to
say about how in this anti-romantic, not
to say sceptical, age I 'dealt with the
poetry in Shakespeare'. How I do, I asked,
or how does one? 'How you do'.

Deal with . . . I'm not sure I do; 'approach'
might be easier to answer. The truth for me
is . . . in speech or in poetry, meaning is
everything – and good dialogue, with its

*own intention, its soul, creates its own
rhythm. So in Shakespeare as in everything, I suppose, I first seek out that
meaning, the 'soul' of what I think is to
be said, and expect to pick up its internal
rhythm. Then I interpret that rhythm, just
as I imagine a musician interprets the soul
of a piece of music playing 'rubato'.*

*In the late-sixties, after I'd appeared in a
few films, I was invited to take part in a
BBC Omnibus programme about W.H.
Auden along with three actors from the
RSC. We were to render the poems, and
I was thrilled and terrified to be in such
august company. I'd always supposed there
was a special 'voice' for speaking poetry –
that a sort of magical cloak of great beauty
descended and enwrapped the utterances of
certain lucky people so they made glorious
sound. I was pretty sure I didn't have it.
With a few days off from filming, I went
up to be with my actor husband who was
playing the Belgrade Theatre in Coventry.
While he rehearsed I set off for the hills to
learn the poems and discover this 'voice'.
Wind rose, rain lashed down as, in despair
of the cloak descending, I railed through
the poems at the elements. The carefully-
modulated Susannah I'd been trying so
hard to be was tossed to the wind; I felt
I was breaking the sound barrier, felt an
extraordinary sense of liberation as the
words howled out (often quite against their*

clear intent) and it came to me: 'Auden's needing to say something, he's meaning something, the poet wants to be listened to – he's communicating!', and what I had to do was to discover and reveal all his thought.

And that's what I think about Shakespeare. Whether in prose or blank verse, you have to discover and reveal all his characters' thought. If you have a good ear and have been well-taught; and if you love language and have a natural sense of rhythm – and what good actor doesn't, hasn't? – the words will take care of themselves. Arcane, outmoded some of them may sometimes seem 'in these days', but the emotions, the engine that drives these words, are as relevant now as they ever were, and as universal: you just mean them. You just say them.

Antony and Cleopatra

The Egyptian army has once more deserted
Antony, this time in a land battle against the
Romans. The defeated Antony has blamed
Cleopatra who hides in her Monument,
sending word that she is dead, whereupon he
falls on his sword and is carried to the
Monument to die in her arms. Rather than fall
into Roman hands, she too, decides for death
with the aid of a poisonous snake, taking her
waiting women, Charmian and Iras, with her.

CLEOPATRA

Give me my robe, put on my crown: I have
Immortal longings in me; now no more
The juice of Egypt's grape shall moist this lip
Yare, yare, good Iras; quick. Methinks I hear
Antony call: I see him rouse himself
To praise my noble act; I hear him mock
The luck of Caesar, which the gods give men
To excuse their after wrath: husband, I come:
Now to that name my courage prove my title!
I am fire and air; my other elements
I give to baser life. So, have you done?
Come then and take the last warmth of my lips.
Farewell, kind Charmian; Iras, long farewell.

Iras falls and dies

Have I the aspic in my lips? Dost fall?
If thou and nature can so gently part,

The stroke of death is as a lover's pinch
Which hurts, and is desir'd. Dost thou lie still?
If thus thou vanishest, thou tells the world
It is not worth leave-taking. . . . This proves me base:
If she first meet the curled Antony,
He'll make demand of her, and spend that kiss
Which is my heaven to have. Come, thou mortal
    wretch,
With thy sharp teeth this knot intrinsicate
Of life at once untie; poor venomous fool,
Be angry and dispatch . . . Peace, peace!
Dost thou not see my baby at my breast
That sucks the nurse asleep?
As sweet as balm, as soft as air, as gentle –
O Antony! (*Dies.*)

Act V, Scene 2

Macbeth

Here are two further speeches by Lady
Macbeth, who exemplifies both love turned
awry, and love of power. In this first, she has
just learned through a message from her
husband, of the witches' prophecy to him,
'Thou shalt be king hereafter'.

LADY MACBETH

Glamis thou art, and Cawdor; and shalt be
What thou art promis'd. Yet do I fear thy nature;
It is too full of the milk of human kindness
To catch the nearest way; thou wouldst be great,
Art not without ambition but without
The illness should attend it; what thou wouldst highly,
That wouldst thou holily; wouldst not play false
And yet wouldst wrongly win; thou'dst have,
    great Glamis,
That which cries 'Thus thou must do if thou
    would'st have it';
And that which rather thou dost fear to do
Than wishest should be undone. Hie thee hither
That I may pour my spirits in thine ear
And chastise with the valour of my tongue
All that impedes thee from the golden round,
Which fate and metaphysical aid doth seem
To have thee crown'd withal.
Come, you spirits
That tend on mortal thoughts! unsex me here
And fill me from the crown to the toe top-full
Of direst cruelty; make thick my blood,

Stop up the access and passage to remorse,
That no compunctuous visitings of nature
Shake my fell purpose, nor keep peace between
The effects and it! Come to my woman's breasts
And take my milk for gall, you murdering ministers
Wherever in your sightless substances
You wait on nature's mischief! Come, thick night
And pall thee in the dunnest smoke of hell,
That my keen knife see not the wound it makes
Nor heaven peep through the blanket of the dark
To cry 'Hold, hold!'

Act I, Scene 5

*Duncan, Banquo, Lady Macduff and her
children have all been slaughtered in Macbeth's
wavering determination – which has been
inexorably propped up by his wife – to secure
and retain the crown. While Macbeth sets off
to quell a revolt by Macduff and Duncan's son
Malcolm, Lady Macbeth, tormented by guilt, is
discovered walking in her sleep by her waiting-
woman and a doctor . . .*

LADY MACBETH

Yet here's a spot . . . Out, damned spot! Out, I say!
One; two; why, then 'tis time to do't. Hell is
murky! Fie, my lord, fie! A soldier and afeard?
What need we fear who knows it when none can
call our power to account? Yet who would have
thought the old man to have had so much blood
in him? . . .

The Thane of Fife had a wife: where is she now? What! Will these hands ne'er be clean? No more o' that, my lord, no more o' that: you mar all with this starting.

... Here's the smell of the blood still: all the perfumes of Arabia will not sweeten this little hand. Oh! oh! oh! ...

Wash your hands, put on your night-gown; look not so pale. I tell you yet again, Banquo's buried; he cannot come out on's grave.

To bed, to bed: there's knocking at the gate. Come, come, come, come, give me your hand. What's done cannot be undone. To bed, to bed, to bed.

Act V, Scene 1

Coriolanus

This speech of Volumnia's strikes me as a strong possible alternative to Queen Margaret. Although I love playing Margaret!

Volumnia, a fierce Roman matriarch, has raised her son Coriolanus to think of himself as invincible. His defeat of Rome's neighbours, the Volsces, elevates him to hero-status, and he becomes a kind of killing machine on behalf of the Roman state.

But he is no politician. When he openly despises the commoners, they reject him as consul and send him into exile. Coriolanus defects, embittered and vengeful, to his own old enemies the Volsces, and returns as leader of their army to devastate Rome.

Among those who must perish are his family – wife Virgilia, small son Martius, and his mother Volumnia. Mother-love and country-love jostle for place when Volumnia humbles herself before Coriolanus, this paradigm of pride of her own creation, to beg mercy for the city.

This is another take on mercy, reasoned, concrete, but equal in passion to Isabella's or Portia's, and extraordinary to hear from this woman who has raised son and grandson to tear the wings off butterflies.

VOLUMNIA:

Should we be silent and not speak, our raiment
And state of bodies would bewray what life
We have led since thy exile. Think with thyself
How more unfortunate than all living women
Are we come hither, since that thy sight, which should
Make our eyes flow with joy, hearts dance with
    comforts,
Constrains them weep, and shake with fear and
    sorrow;
Making the mother, wife, and child to see
The son, husband, and the father tearing
His country's bowels out. For how can we,
Alas! how can we for our country pray,
Whereto we are bound, together with thy victory,
Whereto we are bound? Alack, or we must lose
The country, our dear nurse, or else thy person,
Our comfort in the country – for either thou
Must as a foreign recreant, be led
With manacles through our streets, or else
Triumphantly tread upon thy country's ruin
And bear the palm for having bravely shed
Thy wife and children's blood! For myself, son
I purpose not to wait on Fortune till these wars
Determine. If I cannot persuade thee
Rather to show a noble grace to both parts
Than seek the end of one, thou shalt no sooner
March to assault thy country than to tread –
Trust to't, thou shalt not – on thy mother's womb
That brought thee to this world.

Nay, go not from us thus! Our suit
Is that you reconcile them: so the Volsces

May say 'This mercy have we showed', the Romans
'This have we receiv'd', and each in either side
Give the all-hail to thee and cry 'Be bless'd
For making up this peace!' Speak to me son!
Think'st thou it honourable for a noble man
Still to remember wrongs? He turns away:
Down, ladies, let us shame him with our knees.
To his surname Coriolanus 'longs more pride
Than pity to our prayers. Down: an end;
This is the last: so we will home to Rome
And die among our neighbours. – Nay, behold us!

Act V, Scene 3

The Absence of
Mother-Daughter Relationships
in Shakespeare . . .

*When I was looking for my women, it puzzled
me very much to find in none of the plays a
mother-daughter relationship that was pivotal,
or even explored. Mother-son, father-son,
father-daughter relationships abound, but
mothers and daughters? Mistress Page and
Anne, Hermione and Perdita, Lady Capulet
and Juliet, 'All's Well''s Widow and Diana were
all I could turn up. Loving inter-reaction –
inter-reaction of any kind – between a mother
and a daughter receives very short shrift, and
I wonder why.*

*Given Shakespeare's innumerable feisty mothers
of sons, that he never wrote of them in relation
to their daughters can't simply be down to
women's, or even mothers', position in the
society of his time . . . Perhaps the absence
reflects his perception of his wife Anne's
relationship with their daughters, Susanna and
Judith? Or perhaps – absentee travelling-
player-father that he was – he has simply
turned everything on its head, and it's his own
absent relationship with his daughters he is not
writing; perhaps it was only fantasized
paternity to his daughters he could bear?*

*Whatever the truth, you can't help feeling that
the absence of the seminal mother-daughter
relationship in the work of this man who wrote
all things about all people must have been
more than mere oversight.*

If, however, Rosalind, Miranda, Hermia,
Beatrice, Portia and so many others are
motherless, there are the heroines with proxy,
or would-be mothers, women whose love for
another in their orbit is maternal: Emilia's for
Desdemona; I've already spoken of what I feel
to be Gertrude's sense of 'daughter-lessness';
and (a 'Possible', of course), the Nurse in
'Romeo and Juliet', wet-nurse to Juliet until
she was three, who remembers in Act I with
all the bright, sharply-etched tenderness of a
mother the day the little girl was weaned and
'waddled all about', is another.

And there is the Countess of Roussillon in 'All's
Well That Ends Well', mother of Bertram, and
'foster' mother of Helena.

All's Well That Ends Well

*The Countess loves her ward Helena, daughter
of a celebrated physician, as if she were her
own child; and Helena, the Countess discovers,
is in love with Bertram, the Countess's son . . .*

COUNTESS OF ROUSSILLON

Even so it was with me when I was young;
If ever we are nature's, these are ours; this thorn
Doth to our rose of youth rightly belong;
Our blood to us, this to our blood is born;
It is the seal and show of nature's truth,
Where love's strong passion is impress'd in youth:
Her eye is sick on't: I observe her now.
You know, Helen, I am a mother to you – nay,
      a mother:
Why not a mother? When I said 'a mother'
Methought you saw a serpent: what's in 'mother'
That you start at it? I say I am your mother;
And put you in the catalogue of those
That were enwombed mine: 'tis often seen
Adoption strives with nature, and choice breeds
A native slip to us from foreign seeds;
You ne'er oppress'd me with a mother's groan,
Yet I express to you a mother's care.
God's mercy, maiden! Does it curd thy blood
To say I am thy mother? What's the matter,
Why, that you are my daughter? Pale again?
My fear hath catch'd your fondness: now I see
The mystery of your loneliness, and find

Your salt tears' head: now to all sense 'tis gross
You love my son. Invention is asham'd,
Against the proclamation of thy passion,
To say thou dost not, therefore tell me true –
But tell me then 'tis so, for look, thy cheeks
Confess it, th' one to th'other.

Act I, Scene 3

*Helena has cured the apparently-dying King
of France with a healing potion. She names,
and is granted, her reward – marriage to the
unwilling Bertram. After the wedding he
immediately leaves for war in Italy, writing to
Helena 'Till I have no wife, I have nothing in
France', and dispatching her back to the
Countess.*

COUNTESS OF ROUSSILLON

(*Reading.*) '*I have sent you a daughter-in-law . . .
I have wedded her, not bedded her; and sworn to
make the "not" eternal . . .* '

This is not well: rash and unbridled boy,
To fly the favours of so good a king!
To pluck his indignation on thy head
By the misprizing of a maid too virtuous
For the contempt of empire!
I have felt so many quirks of joy and grief,
That the first face of neither, on the start,
Can woman me unto't . . .

(*To Helena.*) I prithee, lady, have a better cheer;
If thou engrossest all the griefs are thine,
Thou robb'st me of a moiety: he was my son,
But I do wash his name out of my blood,
And thou art all my child. – Towards Florence is he?
And to be a soldier?
Nothing in France until he have no wife?
There's nothing here that is too good for him
But only she; and she deserves a lord
That twenty such rude boys might tend upon,
And call her hourly mistress. (*To the Gentlemen.*)
I will entreat you, when you see my son,
To tell him that his sword can never win
The honour that he loses . . . Which of them both
Is dearest to me I have no skill in sense
To make distinction. Provide this messenger.
My heart is heavy and mine age is weak;
Grief would have tears, and sorrow bids me speak.

Act III, Scenes 2 and 4

These are the 'Possibles' I've unearthed so far, left with the excitement of knowing there'll be others.

And now, to end the book, an alternative epilogue simply because I love it.

This was the first bit of Shakespeare I learned at school, and Puck was the first Shakespearean role I played. And after the cartwheels and somersaults, terrors and thrills of that performance, I knew without a shadow of doubt that this was the sort of thing I wanted to do with my life.

Puck is not a woman, nor a man either; Puck is androgynous, loves fun . . . and so, it seems to me, is allowed on this last page.

Epilogue

PUCK

If we shadows have offended
Think but this and all is mended
That you have but slumbered here
While these visions did appear.
And this weak and idle theme
No more yielding but a dream . . .

A Midsummer Night's Dream